The Winners' Choice

D1310645

Written by Ana Galan

Illustrated by Christos Skaltsas

PEARSON

ISBN-13: 978-0-328-83274-3
ISBN-10: 0-328-83274-X
5 6 7   18 17 16

It was the end of soccer practice at Las Águilas School. Coach Ramos stood in front of the soccer team.

The team had beaten Los Leones School in the soccer tournament. The golden trophy now sat in the display case in the hall. The school had also won some money.

"I have some more exciting news," Coach Ramos announced.

3

What could it be? The team started talking excitedly.

"Shhhh!" said Coach Ramos. Everyone was quiet.

"I have been speaking to the principal," said Coach Ramos. "She thinks *you* should choose how to spend the prize money."

The children gasped.

"Can we spend it on anything we want?" Luis called out.

"Anything, as long as it's for the school," replied Coach Ramos.

For the rest of the day, all the team could think about was what to do with the money.

"I've got it!" said Carlos. "We could get a soccer field that turns into a swimming pool."

"It could turn into
a skate park too!"
said Gabriela.
    "Yes!" cheered
their teammates.

"I don't think we have *that* much money," said Marta.

"What about a new uniform with socks that glow in the dark?" said Carlos. "That would be so cool!"

"What's wrong with our uniform?" asked Patricia. "I like it how it is."

"I have the best idea!" exclaimed Juan. "A chocolate fountain . . . right in the middle of the field!"

"But that has nothing to do with soccer!" said Patricia.

"Well . . . it could be in the shape of a soccer ball," replied Juan.

Patricia rolled her eyes. "That makes no sense, Juan! What about—" Patricia started to say.

Then she stopped. She felt something move under her feet. "What was that?" she gasped.

Then she felt it again. The ground was shaking. The soccer field was shaking. The entire *city* was shaking!

"It's an earthquake!" cried Coach Ramos.

"Stay calm," instructed Coach Ramos. "Sit down here. Don't go near the building!"

The team crowded together in the middle of the field. They could hear the rumbling and the rattling of the school windows. The earth trembled beneath them.

The shaking lasted a few minutes. Then it stopped.

First Coach Ramos made sure nobody was hurt. Then he called the principal.

"We're safe now," he said to the team. "You were all very brave. The principal said your parents will come to pick you up."

The team waited. They hoped their parents would come quickly.

Patricia was walking home with her mom. She could see the damage the earthquake had caused. Broken glass was everywhere.

Fire trucks and ambulances were zooming down the streets.

People gathered outside, hugging each other.

Patricia and her mom walked
past Los Leones School. Their
soccer field was ruined. There was
a deep crack in the ground
   Patricia turned to her mom.
"I have an idea," she said.

The next day, Patricia told her teammates her idea. Then they all went to see Coach Ramos.

"We know what to spend the money on," said Patricia. "We don't need a chocolate fountain. Or new uniforms. We want to help Los Leones School. Their soccer field was ruined in the earthquake. Our money can help clean it up."

Coach Ramos smiled. "That's a great idea!"

A month later, Las Águilas School was playing against Los Leones School.

Patricia took her position as captain and looked around. Los Leones' field was better than ever! She smiled proudly.

The captain of Los Leones' team shook Patricia's hand.

"Thank you for fixing our field," he said warmly.

The referee blew the whistle and the game began. Everyone cheered.